As I See It

By

Dr. Sudhakar Iyer

INKQUILLS®
FOR THE READERS, BY THE WRITERS

Published by InkQuills Publishing House
www.inkquills.in

First Edition 2025

ISBN: 978-81-982215-4-4

This book is dedicated to my parents

Shri. T.V. Ramamurthi

Smt. R. Kamala

PREFACE

The happenings around us present itself in many shades — sometimes vivid, sometimes muted — and each of us views it through a personal unique lens.

'As I See It' is my attempt to capture and share what comes into focus through mine. Neither is it a manual nor it is a manifesto; It's more like a stroll through my mental attic, where you'll find everything from thoughtful reflections on social happenings to cheeky takes on politics, from movie musings to stinging satire.

These fifty essays meander through a wide landscape and some are rooted in my personal experiences, others in observations, and a few in the irresistible urge to poke fun at the strange ways we humans behave.

At times, you may find the tone thoughtful and reflective; at others, playful and irreverent. That's because life itself isn't uniform or predictable— one moment it makes us think deeply, the next it makes us laugh at its absurdity.

I don't claim to offer universal truths here. What you'll find are my perspectives, shaped by curiosity and a love of storytelling.

In the end, these pages are simply how I make sense of a noisy, colorful, and often weird world. Whether you nod in agreement, shake your head in disbelief, or simply chuckle, I'll consider that my purpose of bringing this collection to you is served.

Dr. Sudhakar Iyer

15th August 2025

The Collection

Gaining Immortality Status 1

The Attire of Spirituality 3

The Price of Impatience! 8

The Paradigm Shift in South Indian Arranged Marriage System! 10

The Humble Rava-Upma! 12

Two Friends 14

The National Mannerism 15

The Thesaurus Treat 16

Beauty of the Masculine 17

Conflict of Loyalties 19

The Hypocritical Debate 22

Melody Queen for the Gods now! 23

Satire on Attire! 25

Purity of Rituals And Offerings! 27

IPL: A Display of Stark Apathy And Insensitivity? 29

'Leader' is A Misnomer in India! 31

Politically Correct Gratitude! 34

The Damned Indian Men! 36

Laughter - Any Medicine? 37

Blown Out of Proportion? 38

We Indians Love Crowds! 40

'Bowry' 42

Holiday - Mark of Respect Or Homage? 43

Sowing And Reaping Karma 44

The Pangs of Withdrawal Symptoms 47

The Urge for Corruption 50
Whom to Change And Why? 53
The Innocent Indian Wives! 55
Modern Housewives Salary Quotient! 57
Enlightening Insight from a Wife! 63
Issue of Food Wastage 66
Democrazy 68
Detached Or Insensitive? 69
Adding Insult to Injury! 71
Poverty of Integrity! 72
Fixing Answerability! 75
Government's Public Spending 77
State Control of Hindu Temples - Fundamental Rights violation? 79
Much Ado about Nothing! 81
Role of the Almighty 83
The Delusional Claustrophobia 85
The Appeal in the Repeal!!! 87
The Slow Death of Our Collective Conscience? 90
Using Democratic Right to Kill Itself. 92
From Right to Pray to Fight to Pray 95
Thick Skinned Conscience! 99
The Language Politics 101
Politics And Conscience 103
The Failed Population Policy 104
Divide And Rule 106

Gaining Immortality Status

The desire to be loved and be remembered is a normal human tendency. But some people add greed and malice to that feeling desiring to become immortal.

The coming generations will surely remember great singers, scientists, writers even few politicians and business magnets out of their free will and reverence.

On my few visits to different places in Andhra Pradesh, I was actually surprised to find most deities in temples (especially built in the seventies and eighties) and statues at different squares, had the facial image of the actor turned CM N. T. Ramarao (Popularly called NTR). At first it struck me as odd and a bit ridiculous, but slowly it dawned on me that it may have been deliberately done that way - to gain Demi-God status.

In a way NTR not only wanted to indirectly appeal to the people for votes but also ensured that he will be on the firm pedestal for never-ending posterity.

But such things have happened in other times in history too.

Glorious forts and monuments stand testimony to the greatness of the kings and rulers and they are now permanent part of history books. So are the Newtons, Einsteins, Gandhis and even Hitlers who have achieved immortality status.

The top of them all is Leonardo Da Vinci...the invincible indefatigable renaissance icon. His versatility in various fields itself is enough to make him among the greatest in the annals of mankind. But he chose a different path to immortality. The masterpiece Mona Lisa now in the Louvre church in France was a portrait of Da Vinci himself. For centuries every time people cast their eyes with awe.... he quietly smiled looking at them from the portrait. The master artist turned master masquerader in the guise of smiling beauty.

His masterstroke to become immortal came through the burnt image of the Christ in the 'Shroud of Turin'.

The shroud is the most revered relic for the Christians throughout the world because it is believed to have blood stains of Jesus Christ and the image on the shroud is believed to be of Christ.

Forensic tests and carbon dating have proved beyond doubt that the cloth was not more than 500 years old and the image of Christ was a negative exposure of light through a lens on to the silver compound coated cloth of a bust, torso and limbs taken separately and superimposed.

Leonardo Da Vinci was the genius creator of this!

But hold on...How anyone knew how Christ looked...??

Artists used the negative image on the shroud to create life like statue using computer imaging software only to be awestruck that it was none other than Leonardo himself.

So then for the last five hundred years people all over the world who have accepted Jesus to be a long faced, sharp nosed and long-haired messiah was actually the face of Leonardo Da Vinci!!!

The genius artist made use of his knowledge of optics and human anatomy to become the face of Jesus.

What a master chicanery to achieve immortality!!!

The Attire of Spirituality

Living in India, one is fed with a sumptuous meal of spirituality to such an extent that one gets fed up of it. Of all the things or concepts that is confusing or are soaked in muddy puddle in India, spirituality takes the icing. Although I have met a variety of self- proclaimed spiritual gurus, none have been able to describe or explain 'spirituality' with any conviction.

Hypocrisy in India is colourful and even entertaining when it comes to religious topics. As a teacher and author, I always carry this shame that I have never been able to have a clear thought on spirituality and doubts on the subject come as chain reaction.

One of my friends took me to a Guru whom he revered to such an extent that he considered him to be the ultimate source of spiritual knowledge and a deep interpreter of Hindu philosophies. After a patient hearing, I told him, being a teacher there was an impulsive urge in me to talk and not so much to listen. He smiled and said - one who has ventured into the horizons of spirituality is never flustered with any question thrown at him.

I started - if spirituality can be truly understood only when we are liberated from all the shackles of materialism they why is he sporting a long beard and always wears a white dress. How does a dress code matter to a spiritually enlightened person?

He was lost in thought and I was lost in reading his reaction. My friend's reverence got punctured for his Guru was all at sea.

I returned home fairly satisfied having checkmated another hypocrite. Indians are easily fleeceable when it comes to talks on spirituality. We have the uncanny sense of accepting everything as correct if it comes from the mouth of a spiritual leader. When we are thoroughly confused about something, we say it is beyond our understanding. In case of spirituality, it is not so. We are confused because nobody has given or can give a comprehensive doubt free explanation to the spirituality concept.

One another guru said - true spiritualism is to set the Atma (read spirit) free from all vanities, not to confine it by any walls of worldly desires and the rightful path is through meditation and rigorous penance. I asked then why does he keep doing pujas (procedural veneration of deities) day in and day out when it is definitely not a path to attain spirituality as it contradicts his own idea of spiritualism. Again, clean bowled!

You can't reach Delhi if you board a Chennai bound train. Right?

We poor Indians have always been gullible. Anybody wears a 'baba' dress and we are convinced of his spirituality. He will roam around in the costliest luxury cars, travel business class, use latest mobiles, use satellite communication to air his elementary talks, walk on red carpet, eat things made out of pure ghee etc. and just because he wears white dress and has a long beard, he is assumed to symbolize spirituality. Not to forget knowing few obscure Sanskrit verses and some knowledge of yoga adds up to your spiritual personality.

So, is there an attire for looking or feeling spiritual???

If a judge were to pronounce a judgment wearing a Bermuda and banian, it will be unacceptable although what matters is what he is going to say. Similarly, people want doctors to look like doctors more than their proficiency. They want lawyers to look like lawyers wearing black gown and white tab. Although these are codified uniforms but it has now become a part of their personalities and profession.

In India you change your get up the moment- you are elected even in a local municipal election - white kurta-pajama and Gandhi Topi (cap), you become a daughter in-law - Dulhan getup, you get a corporate job - formal shirt and pant, you become a priest - dhoti and shirtless etc.

The same applies to a person who wants to talk about spirituality - his getup is important more than anything else. That explains why all religious gurus and satellite babas appear to be in a uniform with slight variation to give them a distinct identity. I have never come across a clean shaven, T shirt -Jeans clad spiritual guru at least in India. As they say, first impression is the last impression - a baba or a guru must look like one in the first place.

Obsession with anything is an obstruction in the path to spirituality yet our spiritual gurus are obsessed with their looks.

Their white cloak is soaked in all the colours of vanity, innocent and unintentional hypocrisy and desire for material pleasures camouflaged in the long beard. I am told there is TRP ratings for Babas too based on their popularity ratings and discourse attendance. Modern spiritual gurus ride on pure economics for they have to maintain huge ashrams and spend a hell on their image marketing and for all that they have to get into commercial businesses. All these material support is necessary to establish the fact that these are not necessary for attaining spirituality.

To me, 'Spirituality is trying to get liberated from the things that stop us seeing the universal consciousness. Absolute spirituality is a myth. Because unless we nourish our mind and body with material food, it will not have the strength to stop worrying about it. It is something like you can be free of toothache only when your teeth are in good condition. Your mind will become capable of liberation only when the body is fed with material things to keep it fit.

Most people in India think any activity associated with religion, God and charity is spiritual. To list what people think as spiritual in India can be a nerve-wracking task albeit exciting.

To name a few-

• Giving alms to the poor

• Visiting many temples

• Conducting pujas or veneration rituals

• Reading Holy Books, or reading epics

• Garlanding deities

• Distributing free food or Prasad

• Wearing Saffron coloured shawls with OM or some God's name written on it, wearing vermilion on forehead etc., the list is actually endless.

In spite of doing so many material rituals and deeds many people think the path to spirituality is actually "detachment" from these activities.

What a paradox!!!

We keep doing a thing just because we want to become capable of getting rid of it.

My spiritual gurus are the poor herbivorous animals - mute and divine!!! They see me as a human being, that's it. And I see them as spiritual beings untouched by any lust for any material possessions or craving for spirituality status.

The only time we humans were truly spiritual and pure was when we were infants. After that it is impossible to attain that state of mind!!!

The Price of Impatience!

Remaining busy is different from remaining impatient.

Captain Mahendra Singh Dhoni showed patience and won many cups than other captains who were aggressive and impatient.

The art of being patient for anything, is rapidly getting extinct.

I am reminded of a Sant Kabir Doha-

धीरे धीरे रे मना,
धीरे सब कुछ होय,
माली सींचे सौ घड़ा,
ऋतु आए फल होय।

Unless we appreciate that everything need not and will not happen at the pace that we want, life is always going to be stressful. Today, small children, teenagers, youths and even old people want everything quick and fast. Instant achievement or gratification is what satisfies them.

If people fall ill, they want quick fix allopathic medicines...

If there are exams, students want some crash course...

Youths want to achieve everything by 25....

Newly married women want their husbands to become Narayan Murthy or Elon Musk within two years.

People want everything fast--faster flights, faster trains etc. Nobody has the patience to reach the destination slowly.

Even an unemployed bloke feels he is wasting money by standing in the railway queue.

We have become impatient in everything - we watch many TV channels simultaneously; don't apply our concentration on any one program.

If we start getting what we want instantly, we develop impatience, it slowly grows as an irresistible impulse and we feel miserable and mortified and our blood pressure shoots up every time we have to wait for something or someone.

So, if we are impatient, we feel stressed and that leads to more mental health issues and more impatience. It is a vicious cycle!

People have no patience to listen to long classical music or concerts. People don't watch classical dances or learn classical instruments anymore as these require lot of patience.

By being impatient we miss so many beautiful things in life.

The price we pay for impatience in the long run is immense - it direly affects our physical health, mental health and relationships. We become grumpy, irritating and look flustered and frustrated all the time.

The sooner we learn the art of being 'patient', the lesser we have chances of becoming 'patients'.

Many of my regular readers complain....my write ups are very long and they stop reading mid-way. That's precisely the malaise we all are suffering from - Impatience!

The Paradigm Shift in South Indian Arranged Marriage System!

I have memories of scenes from Hindi films of seventies, Eighties and Nineties where the police or the aggrieved in- laws would curse the bridegroom for asking dowry. They would say 'Dahej ke liye' ladki se shadi karna ek paap hai (It is a sin to marry a girl for dowry)

Institution of marriage is not a market - Agreed!

Fast forward to 2025...

Look at the many advertisements in matrimonial columns for prospective bridegrooms in TN.

You will just be zapped and appalled at the Topsy-turvy of the scenario.

Required bridegrooms - salary minimum yearly 15L package.

US settled preferred.

Own house minus in-laws.

Gone are the days when girls were more interested in knowing -

- Education
- Personality
- Habits
- Mannerisms
- Family background
- Vices etc. of the alliance.

Now they care a damn about what his vices are, character or even the dignity of his profession, the only criteria is 'Salary'.

No wonder men and women in TN looking out for marriage alliance with unreasonable demands remain unmarried well into their forties.

Most educated young girls in TN are bugged by consumerism and possessed by the ghost of materialism.... a 'Husband' for them is nothing but an ATM and credit card. Demanding a six-figure earning 'Husband' is a Reverse-Dowry.

You might just have a feeling that I have exaggerated it beyond what common sense warrants.

Nay!

Just check out for few matrimonial advertisements by family of Tamil girls, I am sure you will appreciate that I broached this topic.

The Humble Rava-Upma!

Of late stand-up comedians and public speakers are using 'Rava-Upma' as an analogy to things that are degraded and valueless. Rava-Upma is used almost like a 'Chutney' in every humour conversation in Tamil Nadu.

However, Rava-Upma is still liked by millions who see it as a variety alternative to Idli-Dosa in the morning breakfast.

Rava-Upma invokes fond memories - my mother used to make exceptional vegetable Rava-Upma for breakfast during school times. I still don't know how she managed to get that crispy Upma in the bottom of the alloy vessel, that we enjoyed scrapping and eating.

Easy to make and easy to digest the humble Rava-Upma is part of South Indian cuisine for centuries. It is considered as a budget option in functions and celebrations. The mere presence of it suggests that the programme is a low profile-low budget one. There is a clear conspiracy against Rava-Upma by the entertainment industry. The derision is built up to such an extent that the younger generation has started feeling a kind of wretchedness in consuming Rava-Upma.

For people who believe in 'Simple Living and High Thinking' Rava-Upma is an eternal companion.

Why attach social status to simple dishes?

Why make it a prestige issue?

Be it simple Rava-Upma or dal-rice or thayir-sadam or even a simple vada-pav, they can be a gourmet to millions like me!

There's no shame in being simple and absolutely no shame in liking things that are simple.

Why bother the roving eyes when you choose Rava-Upma?

You may not gourmandize Rava-Upma on a daily basis but once a week we shouldn't forget this humble delicacy!

Two Friends

When the news of Mr. Gopinath's death reached Ramaswamy Naicker, he found it very difficult to react. Gopinath had been his friend for over a decade and he ought to feel bad about his demise; but Gopinath's challenge to Naicker made the news almost a laughing stock. Gopinath was a staunch believer in God and Naicker was a celebrated atheist. Being members of many social organizations, both were great friends but Gopinath had intense aversion towards Naicker's atheistic views. Naicker spared no opportunity to ridicule Gopinath's eccentric ways of appeasing some of his favourite Gods. Gopinath visited Sabari malai, Tirupati, Rameshwaram, Madurai etc. with such regularity that it seemed he spent all his earnings on his Gods. His family was not much pleased with his over enthusiastic pious behaviour. He was so much God fearing as if God had no other duty in the 'Cosmos' but to keep an eye on what he does. Every time he visited temples, he sincerely prayed for the well -being of his family but he never did anything for their betterment. On many occasions Gopinath and Naicker had heated debates. Naicker riled him to such an extent that he even recommended some of his Gods to punish him. Gopinath emphatically remarked that he would enjoy a long and healthy life while Naicker will meet an unceremonious end very early.

What ultimately happened is that Gopinath passed away at the age of 61 and Ramaswamy Naicker lived upto age 96. No wonder, God takes away his beloved people early.

The National Mannerism

The all-famous habit of spitting is very special to the tropical countries. We find people spitting everywhere and thoroughly enjoying the act. The illiterates and the ignorant take it as their privilege and have painted the corners of the staircases with modern art. Indians are the leaders in the art of spitting; they have developed various styles of spitting and have taken it to greater heights in the society. Spitting is synonymous with the expression of contempt and has been used to a good effect in Indian films.

What is surprising is that people have not spared any place in the town; the cinema theatres, government buildings, compound walls, parks, foot paths etc. you name it and there you will find the mosaic of reddish brown 'paan'. As it has become a glorious tradition among the people, it will simply be a futile effort to impose any penalty or any other restriction on spitting. On the contrary, social groups should come forward and hold spitting competitions to encourage the skill and style of spitting. The government should declare 'spitting' as a national habit and should announce some awards. Spitting spreads diseases and keeps the medical teams alert, (or else they will be bored without much work). There is much more to our habit of spitting than we may imagine, what is needed is a bit of research in this regard.

The Thesaurus Treat

The Oxford Dictionary is an ocean of knowledge, the depth of which increases the more you dive into it. A browsing through the pages of the dictionary is enough to send the reader into a different realm of pleasure. Many are yet to discover the romance in reading the dictionary; they have always thought it to be a reference book for unknown words. In fact, a dictionary addict would agree that there is no parallel to the Pulchritude of a dictionary. The etymology takes you through the exciting evolution of 'English'; it makes you relive the course through which the language has run, taking sediments from many languages. The class of words provides the reader with the intricacies of 'grammar' and the derivative words are authentic evidence of the influence of other languages on 'English'.

Going through the words page by page gives an ineffable thrill and kindles an insatiable desire for more. The dictionary is probably the only book in the world, flawless and meticulous in all respects and there lies its ethereal beauty. Blessed is he who is a dictionary addict; for only he can realise the enlightenment that the dictionary bestows.

Beauty of the Masculine

Once a famous Greek philosopher haranguing on the majestic look of the lion, the imposing elegance of the male elephant, the imperial strides of the tiger, the colour burst of the peacock, the magnificence of the male crow, the raging romp of the rhino, echoing call of the male frog, the royal crown of the cock, when he suddenly remembered that all the examples that he cited were male. He spontaneously exclaimed 'beauty of the masculine is divine'. He made an observation that the male species outclassed the female when it came to beauty, strength and grace. The same holds true to human beings. If the most beautiful woman on the earth stood next to a statuesque handsome young man (a Greek God like figure), she will be nowhere in comparison; the man will be the cynosure of all eyes. Although this thought may not be endorsed by many, it is a design of nature.

The philosopher opined that the beauty of men apart from their physique, lies is the versatility of their personalities. Beauty lies in his thoughts and in his creativity. From the times of the epics, the characters and contributions of men have stood the test of time; the creators of great religions- Jesus, Buddha, Mahavir; great philosophers of the world-from Socrates to Gandhi; great scientists of the world-from Galileo to Einstein; great statesmen of the world-from Lincoln to Churchill; great writers from Valmiki to Shakespeare; great film makers of the world from Chaplin to Satyajit Ray; great explorers of the world-from Magellan to Edmund Hillary; great conquerors of the world–from Alexander to Hitler; great musicians of the world-from Tansen to Beethoven, so on and so forth have invariably been men. They rose to the immortal status not by suppressing any women rights but by blossoming the divinity that was ingrained in them. They were all beautiful, the aura of their charm will pervade for centuries to come. One who considers this point of view as chauvinistic is not only an asinine but is pusillanimous to truth.

Conflict of Loyalties

We Indians are different from almost all the citizens of the world. Even the world's greatest psychologists have not been able to stereotype us. So, it is not only difficult for any foreigner to understand us but it is also impossible for us Indians to understand ourselves. Among many reasons for this is that our loyalty has many tentacles so it moves and flutters in many directions often getting entangled and causing heartburn to us.

Quoting few instances will give you a clear idea of what is being stated.

We all wear colours of different loyalties.

a) Loyalty towards nation

b) Loyalty towards the state to which we may originally belong.

c) Loyalty towards religion, caste, linguistic groups etc.

d) Loyalty towards our city or village etc.

e) Loyalty towards profession or work place although rarely.

f) Loyalty towards family and friends etc.

g) Loyalty towards political parties etc.

Now these loyalties are often in conflict and we poor Indians get mentally battered and smothered at such times not knowing which loyalty to adhere.

The nature of our loyalties defines how we perceive and react to socio-political problems of our country. People ask me why Hindus and Non-Hindus especially the Muslims think and react so differently towards the same issues.

The answer lies in different planes of myriad loyalties of both communities.

A Hindu is loyal to Hinduism as well as Indian sovereignty. All the Holy places, the char dhams, the birth places of Gods and temples for Hindus are all in India so his loyalty for his country is here and his religious loyalty is also here. There is no question of conflict of loyalties for Hindus.

Now take the case of Christians and more so Muslims - although as a citizen they are cent percent loyal to India. They are also emotionally and religiously bound by their respective Holy lands and their religious institutional heads in the Vatican and Mecca.

That explains why Indian Muslims remained mum when Saudi attacked Yemen and Saddam attacked Kuwait but they showed huge resentment and anger against US attacking Iran or Afghanistan.

Likewise, many Muslim nations, foreign groups and organizations feel Indian Muslims are an extension of them in India. So, they get flared up whenever our govt. brings any law or ordinance concerning Muslims.

But such emotional support is not available for Hindus as there is no Hindu nation in the world or any country with Hindu majority population. Same is true for Jains and Sikhs as they too have only India as their only country. In case of Buddhists, there are few countries in Asia with sizeable Buddhist population but somehow Indian Buddhists are not emotionally connected to Chinese or Japanese or Burmese and those countries have never meddled in the affairs of Indian Buddhists.

We all should feel for Indian Muslim brothers and sisters as they are torn in the conflict between heart and head and it's actually emotionally draining for them to take sides.

This is precisely why some Muslims feel that the CAA is against their interest.

Even within India we have loyalty conflicts. I have seen many Malayalees, Tamilians, Biharis, Bengalis etc. in Mumbai who have unflagging loyalty and unconditional love for their state. Even if they are born and brought up in Maharashtra most of them still have not become Maharashtrians. That's what I call emotional loyalty. Nothing wrong with that but it will always be a political platform for regional parties to discriminate and seek votes.

Any bill introduced or law made by any Indian government will be detrimental to the one or the other loyalties of one or many groups. And at such times political parties are ever ready with their axes to grind.

The Hypocritical Debate

Many TV anchors I have seen wearing coat-suit-tie and speaking in English about decolonizing India or rather removing the relics. Their clear contention is that the relics or names of buildings represent our slave mindset? Doesn't make sense to me!

In one such debate, there was a hue and cry to rename the Ripon building and Fort St. George the iconic structures in Chennai. But they are simply buildings, Chennai people don't celebrate British rule around it. There is no awe in that!

We may get rid of names of British names but certainly we cannot erase that from history books, even if we rename Victoria memorial as Mukherjee Museum or something else,

it will still have to be mentioned as such in history books.

The moment we seriously decide to change all that is British in India, we would actually be exposing what all things Britishers did in India in just 200 years of India's 5000 years of history, to the younger generation which actually would defeat our very purpose of erasing colonial memory. It will actually present to the younger generation what the Britishers did which they may never have read in schools or colleges.

The presence of British road names or few statues doesn't at all mean we celebrate colonialism. Common Indians are actually very indifferent to them.

If symbols or relics of colonial past represent our slave mentality then go ahead and get rid of English education and Cricket to start with.

Melody Queen for the Gods now!

There is nothing left to be said about Lataji's life or career. But still, it is irresistible to reiterate. From Nehruji to Modiji, she knew them all and regaled them all. As regards her mellifluous voice, there is no parallel, but larger inspiration is her hard-work and perseverance for seven decades which is mammoth. From Khemchand Prakash to A. R. Rehman, she has sung for all the greats of Indian Cinema. It will not be wrong to say the entire Hindi Film (Melody) Music started from her career and ended with her career in 2000.

In a way, her career span is the actual span of Hindi Film Music. Since year 2000 there has been songs, no doubt, but the 'Melody' is replaced by 'noise'. Lataji could never relate or reconcile with songs without melody.

Every singer has limitations - limitations of genre, limitations of scale-range etc. but Lataji could emote all the 'bhav' or 'ras' that any song demanded. Be it bhajans, ghazals, qawaali, classical, sad songs, happy songs, party songs, cabaret or simply light music, there is no genre in music that she has not touched upon. That's absolutely divine!

On top of that she also managed to tackle competition from singers from 1950s to 2000s.

The great Madan Mohan once said – 'kambakht kabhi besuri nahi hoti' -that's the level of perfection. The connoisseurs have yet to spot a 'wrong note' in the thousands of songs that she rendered. It is difficult to say what is so special that Lata-didi had, that's not there in other female singers like Asha or MS or Chitra or S Janaki etc. But everyone agrees there is an exceptional perfection of 'sur' that may have the 'Divine intervention'.

Of the many glorious contributions by Indians to the world, 'Lataji' is definitely on the top. Times will never be the same, songs will never be the same, and taste of music will never be the same, so for sure there will never be another Lataji!

We all have been fed with the sumptuous rich feast of her melodious songs. It has been an inseparable companion in our journey of life. Now it's Gods turn to enjoy her melody!

Satire on Attire!

Handsome is what handsome does! - so goes a famous saying, but do we really mean it?

The first impression about a person is his attire and first of the first is the footwear that he wears.

While all types of dresses don't suit a person's personality, people do like to try out all varieties defying public opinions.

Then there are lot many factors that influence our perception of a good or suitable dress. In fact, men and women vastly differ in their opinions about whether a particular dress suits a person or not.

What suits a person is a subjective inference.

Especially when it comes to women's opinion about other women's dressing-the opinions depend upon who the other person is and what sort of relation she has with her and how she behaved with her last time etc.

When you ask men, whether a particular dress suits a woman, who is in front of him-he will always say it looks good on her.

In a particular marriage just ask a few ladies about how a particular lady looks on a particular saree-exactly opposite views you will get.

Some will say she looks awesome and some will say it doesn't suit her at all.

Mr. A complimented a woman saying she looked gorgeous on a particular saree. Pat came a sharp reaction from his wife Mrs. A – Huuuuut Makddin disstiye (looking like a monkey) (Don't know which monkey she saw draped in a saree)

Women's opinion about other women's attire-more often than not is warped in envy and less objective.

The fact still remains - if you simply respect or love a person, anything that he / she wears will be impressive!

Purity of Rituals And Offerings!

Come 'Shrawan month' and the series of festivals begin, only to end with 'Tulsi Kalyanam' three months later.

Each festival has its own significance and colour. Not only that there are specific rituals or 'Vidhis' too.

Definitely these are 'man created' and have evolved over the last couple of millennium.

Supposed to be the most pious man in our circle, is our family pundit, whom we refer to as "vadhyaar". He guides us in matters of "puja practices". Over the years many changes have been included in performing pujas or rather improvements to suit our convenience.

While choosing convenience in rituals whether we have diluted or corrupted the practices, is a matter of another debate.

Offering 'neivedhyams' or 'bhog' or 'special edible items' for the Gods has always been a matter of great interest to me since my childhood. I am impressed by the variety of items that we offer to God on each festival. The items are mainly the things that are associated with the particular God whose 'birthday' we celebrate.

Now many Puritans or self-proclaimed religious authorities say that the things for 'neivedhyams' should not be bought from shops that is not acceptable to Gods.

We should prepare the things at home and offer it to God.

Actually, sounds good!

But in the age of outsourcing for convenience, even buying things for 'neivedhyams' or 'bhog' is becoming the order of the day.

For that matter, even the flowers, fruits, coconuts, betel leaves, Arecanuts or supari, camphor etc that we use for puja is also not 'home-made'.

Besides we don't just keep shop made 'pedhas' or 'chaklis' or 'murukku' or 'seedai' for puja, we also keep home-made 'rice', 'payasam', 'vadai', 'avval' 'sakarrai-pongal' etc for neivedhyam. So, what's the fuss about buying a couple of items from the shop?

Offering to help someone is the real offering to God!

And by buying sweets during festivals, we are only helping those poor people who are in the "small scale business of making homemade sweets".

Go ahead and celebrate festivals with a variety of 'neivedhyams'.... make some at home that is possible for you...buy the remaining from shops, no problem!

God is all forgiving!

On a lighter note - even Lord Krishna didn't eat 'vennai' or 'butter' of his own house. He would steal from other houses and eat!

IPL: A Display of Stark Apathy And Insensitivity?

Being apathetic or insensitive has always been in our Indian demeanor.

We have about 35 crore population living below poverty line and that is equal to the entire population of the US.

Not that we were taught in school to be indifferent, it grows with us.

We ignore beggars sitting in bee-line outside temples.

We comfortably eat ice-creams, vada-pavs, and sandwiches on roadside stalls with small starving beggars staring at our face many a times.

One sight has remained permanently etched in my memory - it was during one of my cousin's marriage in a small Tamil Nadu town. Lunch there is served on banana leaf. People who finished lunch were asked to wash hands behind the 'mandap' or 'pandal'. I went there to wash my hands. A large drum was kept filled with water. When I picked up the mug, I saw a lungi clad man took all the left-over banana leaves in a large basket and dumped it in the large garbage bin. Immediately few small beggars crowded over the bin and started sifting to find some left over vadas or ladoos. My heart wrenched. I had never felt so cringe!

That's how we Indians are, we carry on with our celebrations no matter what gory things happen all around us.

We move on.

The word 'aage jao' is a trite amongst us Indians.

In Indian metro-cities, we find slums just outside a multistoried building...the rich and famous living in that building care a damn for the street destitute or urchins living by the gutter.

No other country in the world can 'boast' of such an 'earth to sky' inequalities of income and wealth as that in our country...I am using the word 'boast' because we are no longer ashamed of it!

The BPL people have always been sustaining a wretched life but the remaining 75% have always lived a life - unconcerned and insensitive to them as if they are not a part of India.

IPL during this pandemic is a mundane affair. There are many people like me who are seeing the matches as the beggars see us munching in front of them.

I don't know about other viewers but I feel in this 2022 IPL, many foreign players are slowly feeling guilty of playing, when the whole country is reeling under the pandemic.

It is slowly dawning on the players, when all kinds of celebrations are virtually stopped in the country, why the hell is IPL going on?

Is it any kind of entertainment anymore???

For us Indians, we are used to such things, it doesn't matter a bit-money is everything!

'Leader' is A Misnomer in India!

Of the many terms that are misnomers in India-the word 'leader' is the most striking misnomer.

The word leader is used so loosely by us people as well as the media that it has totally lost its genuine sense.

Anyone is called a leader today.

In a small locality there may be many good doctors, engineers, professors and other intellectuals but some dada with proved criminal credentials becomes the local corporator and assumes the self-proclaimed title 'leader'.

Same goes for many MLAs and MPs.

My leader from a party is an utterly corrupt fellow, gets convicted in a scam...comes out serving a jail sentence but still he is my leader. People who follow news don't need examples to be quoted. Examples are too many in every party.

How can a person with poor intellect and integrity be a leader of educated people???

Such type of so-called leaders with poor morality, money-hounding appetite, inflated egos and intoxicated in the 'spirit' of power are unfortunately found in all parties in India.

They have been allowed to reach such a position by our own constitution.

There are no loopholes in our laws - there are loop-doors!

Or else how do you justify that nearly 40% of the Lok Sabha MPs have criminal records.

We are lamenting full throttle about the dismal state of our health care system or education system, but isn't that too much to expect from our 'leaders' who themselves are intellectually incapable of comprehending any crisis, let alone providing solutions?

From so many absurd provisions in our constitution let me pull out one simple example.

Look at the qualification criteria to become corporator, MLA or MP -practically no qualifications required.

You simply need to be born in India, attained age 25-that's it! You may be a top-class idiot or a donkey - doesn't matter!

You don't need to search such people anywhere. Just put on the Lok Sabha TV during a parliament session.

Now take the case of a primary school teacher's job or a clerical job in an office. We scrutinize, we filter, we interview, we take demo, we even do their health checkup We put them on probation and then the person is kept on job but for such an important position / job like MLA or MP nothing is required absolutely!

I remember a case, when my college friend was rejected for a railway clerk's job as he was a bit 'underweight'. Now he is a corporator in Ulhasnagar.

You may ask why this has been going on for over 75 years -simply because if amendment is made requiring qualifications or competence then 80% of the current breed of corrupt and incompetent politicians will be thrown out. Why then they would bring amendments to axe their own feet??

Who becomes a leader in India??

Anyone whose father has been a leader, by default becomes a leader.

Anyone who has high level criminal background and can manage police.

Anyone who is not capable of any other dignified career.

Anyone who has money power, muscle power coupled with basest morality and integrity.

I can't understand how much foolish we can be to expect good administration from such 'men of straw'. If we want to change or improve India in the real sense not just in GDP terms, then many drastic changes have to be made in our constitution, in order to pave way to clean good leaders cum administrators. But that is a big 'IF'

Till then we are free to abuse the current crop of 'leaders' elected by us and derive sadistic pleasure!

Politically Correct Gratitude!

It is a human nature to feel grateful. I will put it this way- it is a sign of a good cultured human being to show gratitude towards people who helped us to achieve success or helped us at times of adversity.

But in India, we have to be careful while expressing gratitude.

It needs to be politically correct!

For instance, take the case of Sachin, yes, the Tendulkar, I don't know any other Sachin.

He is the poster boy for obedient pupils.

Every time people appreciate him for his achievement, he would express his gratitude towards God, his parents, his elder brother Ajit and above all his teenage coach Ramakant Achrekar. It stops at that.

I can't stop thinking, it is the game of cricket that made Sachin. What would he be if he wouldn't be playing cricket?

Why he has never shown his gratitude towards Britishers who introduced cricket in India or for that matter to those who invented or developed cricket in England?

Simply because it is not politically correct.

Same thing we can see -

Film actors and singers have never uttered a word about Thomas Alwa Edison who invented recording.

Railway employees never show gratitude towards Britishers for introducing railways.

Policemen and defence people never show gratitude towards Britishers for having introduced the system.

Electricity is our lifeline but have we ever bothered to show any gratitude towards the person who invented it.

Same goes for computers, medicines, vehicles, TV, internet etc. We have never shown any gratitude towards the inventors who made our lives so much comfortable.

Like expressing gratitude has to be politically correct, even criticism has to be politically correct.

We readily criticize the atrocities committed during the British rule but never utter a word about the atrocities done during the Mughal rule.

We can clearly see this in political circles too. If I am a congressman / NCP / TMC supporter etc. It is never politically correct to show gratitude towards something that Modi Govt. does, even if I am reaping benefits from it. If I am a muslim, appreciating Modi and co. is not just politically incorrect but also religiously incorrect.

So much rigidity and intolerance has crept into our assessment of a thing that we don't dare to express our genuine gratitude even if we feel it somewhere in the corner of our heart.

In India, a rose flower always stinks if it is in our opposition's garden!

I hope the great living legends of cricket read this and at least they acknowledge -

I am what I am due to the people who brought cricket to India.

Believe me, that's going to be tough ask!

The Damned Indian Men!

Since January 2020, in India, the stats reveal that Indian men have been more vulnerable to Covid-19. They have fallen ill more frequently than women, and their death rates too have been higher.

Indian men are 'yamraj's' favourite. Whether it be any rail accident or plane crash or mine deaths or pandemic deaths, men have always been in his priority list.

A small survey will satisfy everyone's curiosity about this. While most of our grandmothers are alive, our grandfathers are only seen on the wall-photos.

Even corona is biased towards Indian women.

It attacks men and leave them gasping for breath while it simply visits some aunty-bodies by error of address and then leaves them with more strong antibodies.

What is the secret? Well, it is still a secret.

Men's lives in India have an ever-dangling dagger on the head, with death lurking all around. While women get protected by virtue of being a woman and also by being in the confines of their homes or offices.

God's Nature and Indian society cares a damn for Indian men. They arrive in great numbers and they depart in great numbers, leaving the women aghast rather than grateful for being an Indian woman.

Laughter - Any Medicine?

We have often heard laughter is the best medicine but have we ever bothered to gather stats as to what is the average life expectancy of a person who is naturally humorous and takes everything lightly.

In recent times, two great comedians from Tamil Nadu - Vivek and Crazy Mohan died of massive cardiac arrests. They were jolly good personalities in both reel life and real life.

Being humorous didn't give any longevity to them.

Can humour actually guarantee a disease free - long life?

Is it a medicine at all?

On the contrary, instances galore of mean-minded, wicked and sadistic people and people with political and social crimes, living a long 90+ age. Most politicians in India indulge in hardcore-cruel activities and still live a long life. Is being 'Dusht' a pre-requisite for longevity? The correlation needs to be researched with proper data.

Some might say-

My so and so uncle or grandmother or grandfather lived 90+ and they were good people. They may be small exceptions, otherwise we would have known them when they are ripe old and completely mellowed down. They would have been diametrically opposite in their hey-days.

Although I cannot leave being humorous, that's a genetic inheritance, it is still baffling to think why comedians die early?

Seriously a humorous doubt!

Blown Out of Proportion?

What is the right dose of a particular news is always debatable.

In the last few years, we have seen some news shown for the whole day on TV or talked about excessively in the social media...like -

1. A small boy falls into the boring well

2. Priyanka Vadra visits Kali Mata Mandir

3. Dhoni has had a new style hair cut

4. Amitabh Bachchan is admitted for routine check up

5. Modiji does some file work during flights.

6. Shahrukh's daughter had to face extreme hardship of walking hundred steps in the sun to reach a building.

So on and so forth...

India is a land of hero-worshippers, unreasonably frenzied. Playing cricket and acting in films are like any other jobs and the people in it are actually human beings in skin and flesh. And like normal human beings they too break laws and indulge in criminal activities.

But the media blows it out of proportion!

The question is - is it justified to keep talking about 'a silly non-consequential news' for the whole day on TV channels?

YES! YES!! YES!!!

When small insignificant things of Actors, cricketers and politicians etc. are shown as great achievements and blown out of proportion, they never complain. When they enjoyed all the unreasonable media attention which was totally undeserving, that time they never complained that media (both regular and social media) are not correct in talking so high about them, they simply enjoyed. So, when some celebrity's son is caught with drugs - and it is blown out of proportion - please don't complain.

Media is a double-edged sword! The so-called Celebrities should be careful in their lives. Everything about them is going to be blown out of proportion.

We Indians Love Crowds!

We Indians like crowds! If there is any place of worship, where there are only handful of devotees waiting to take darshan, we feel this God may not be that powerful or 'alive' as they say. It is only appropriate to throng to places like Tirupati, Vaishnodevi, Shirdi, Ajmer, Velankanni etc. It is a matter of pride for us to state that 'I stood for six hours for the darshan'. I am sure, such people who take too much pain to meet God are bestowed with special blessings!

It a general Indian trait seen everywhere. Same mentality is reflected in other walks of life too.

Right from school admission where people stand in queue to obtain forms, to standing in queues for buying rations.

From standing in queues to buy railway tickets to queues at ATM. We just love standing in queues and test our patience.

One might say we have no option... justified as it may sound but that's not true in most cases. We simply wait for the crowds to build up or we procrastinate doing a thing to such an extent that we are faced with huge crowds at the centers.

Take the case of Corona time, when vaccination started from mid-January 2021, when the cases were less, people were reluctant to get vaccinated but when the second wave was on a rampage, people were seen standing in serpentine queues outside vaccination centers. One of my friends remarked yesterday that he had to stand in the queue for 7 hours at the railway hospital to get the Covishield shot. It is very much likely that those who went to crowded vaccination centers to save themselves from the virus, actually may have brought home the virus.

We people really have great talent to entangle ourselves in precarious situations only to get checkmated!

Aa bail mujhe maar (आ बैल मुझे मार) is not just a humorous Hindi phrase for us - it is our behaviour in most cases.

'Bowry'

Arranged marriages are interesting arrangements. Interesting for its funny nature of contracts between two families. There is an ostensible evolution in the practices of arranged marriages over the years. The system also differs vastly depending on which state or region of India the families belong. In Tamil Nadu, the arranged marriage scenario has changed very much since the IT revolution at the turn of the millennium. When Miss Sowmya Iyer (name changed) and her mother told the boy's parents that they wanted 40 lacs as BOWRY (Dowry paid by the boy), the boy's side reluctantly agreed!

That's what is going around in TN marriage circles especially among Brahmins.

Most parents having marriageable daughters in TN are literally bargaining to the hilt. The going 'bowry' rate is anything between 10 lacs to 50 lacs depending on the profile and earning capacity of the girl. Marriage among Tamil Brahmins (may be in other sects too) is purely a demand-supply market with the equilibrium price largely tilted in favour of girl's family. From giving Dowry to taking Bowry - the marriage practice has turned on its head! Would-be-brides are ruling the roost! What a topsy-turvy!

Holiday - Mark of Respect Or Homage?

Many pseudo intellectuals often say one day holiday declared as 'shraddhanjali' on some great personality's death, results in huge loss to production, finances etc.

Do we need to agree to this view point? The answer is an emphatic 'NO'.

The point in question is the Holiday declared by the Maharashtra Govt. as mourning on Lataji's death.

For many decades people of our generation have enjoyed the songs sung by Lataji. She was very much part of our family functions- no Ganesh festival at home is complete without Lataji's Ganpati songs. Likewise, during birthdays & picnics Lataji's songs entertained us. Her beautiful old melodies were company to many old people languishing at empty homes suffering from 'empty-nest' sickness. Simply listening to her songs of different decades made people nostalgic about the incidents and experiences associated with those songs.

We have 13 days mourning period among Hindus and giving one holiday for a person who not just sang songs for her living but gave immense pleasure by her performances all over the world is not too much to ask. She was a glorious global ambassador of our country.

Holidays are part of Indian culture, an integral part of our way of life. In fact, in many interviews, people ask how many holidays we will get, much before they ask their pay package. One day holiday as a mark of respect to any great legend is not out of place and should not be viewed with the prism of economics.

Sowing And Reaping Karma

From Socrates to Shankacharya, from Thirukkural to Bible we all have been morally fed on the saying 'As you sow, so shall you reap'.

But we find cases- from a street vendor to the president where people keep reaping hundred times more than what they had sown in terms of hard work and investment.

Look at people like thespian Dilip Kumar, Nightingale Lata Mangeshkar, Naushad, Khushwant Singh, G. B. Shaw, M. F. Hussain, S. H. Raza, C. Rajagopalachari, etc who enjoyed the years of stardom when they worked and also enjoyed a long-retired life as a celebrity attaining a legendary status. It is at the pinnacle of contentment that they saw people showering heaps of appreciation and laurels for what they did during their hey days. It is only appropriate that such people have such Karma.

However, there are many such greats who achieved or gave such enduring creations during their productive years and died early. It is as if by a quirk of fate that they didn't get to bask in the glory of their contributions which became prodigious posthumously. People like mathematician Evariste Galois, wizard Ramanujan, Swami Vivekananda, R. D. Burman, Mohd. Rafi, Kishore Kumar, John Keats, Shakespeare, O Henry, Sant Gnaneshwar etc. died so early that they would never have imagined what cult status they have reached in the decades after their death. It is sad indeed that they couldn't reap the fruits of the seeds of ingenuity and originality that they had sown.

Then there is a third category of people whose contribution and achievements are just that it is going to be easily obscured or overcome by people of the next generation but they have reaped colossal amounts of dividends in their retired life extremely disproportionate to what they had sown.

Such people you will easily find in Indian politics, cinema and cricket.

For instance, take the case of a cricketer turned commentator (with due respect to him and his fans) While he was playing, he never hit a century in a single day, it was minimum four sessions. Most matches he played long innings ended in a draw or India lost. Connoisseurs might say he had good technique and temperament but, in a game, the moot point is to win not just to show techniques. So be it. He retired as a batsman who scored the only century in his entire one-day career. His English speaking didn't proceed more than 'sorry', 'thank you', 'please' and his patent expression 'I think' during his post-match interviews in 1970s and 80s.

Post retirement with improved English he donned the role of a commentator and for over three decades he has been around. That is more than double the number of years that he played for India, sixteen.

His commentary (keen listeners would vouch) has not progressed beyond 50 monotonous sentences spoken with the same modulation and drudgery. He still stakes his claim and charges an astronomical sum (not disclosing here) per match for speaking the same thing for the last 38 years. Must be the highest paid professional without anyone noticing it. Does this mean that we never had better players than him in the last three decades or does it mean nobody can speak better English than him?

It's time people like him magnanimously retire and pave way to exciting new commentators. They have already earned much more than what they might have ever imagined for their contribution to cricket or our country. As I said earlier, you will always find many such people in Indian politics, cinema and cricket who have had a prolonged, illustrious and wealthy retired life much more than what their contributions merited!

The Pangs of Withdrawal Symptoms

The other day, during a break between lecture sessions, we were having poha (Maharashtrian breakfast dish), one of my friends said "I can have poha every day, I don't get bored at all, in fact I am addicted, I look forward to have it every morning."

That reminded me of the legendary singer Kishore Kumar. There is an anecdote (hearsay), that he made it a point to remain at home in Mumbai at least every morning to eat poori-bhaji. There were many families around his house and any lady who brought him poori-bhaji at about 9 a.m. would get Rs.100. It was quite a big amount in the seventies and eighties. Kishore Da ate poori-bhaji almost every day. Queer fascination!

Over the years I have come across many people with such strange addictions almost attaining fetish proportion.

To name a few...

- Addiction of fried snacks – Vada-pav, Samosa etc.
- Addiction of chocolates
- Addiction of eating same breakfast or dinner
- Addiction of daily religious rituals
- Addiction of uniform or attire
- Addiction of local train travel
- Addiction of giving lectures or speaking
- Addiction of watching TV serials or sports or News
- Addiction of mobile or social media

- Addiction of simply roaming around the streets
- Addiction of window shopping
- Addiction of meeting friends every evening
- Addiction of partying
- Addiction of gossiping
- Addiction of morning and evening walks etc.
- Other than regular addiction of hot beverages -tea, coffee, cold beverages - aerated drinks, juices etc. and then the hard drinks - beer, whiskey etc.

When we talk of any kind of addiction, even a small break in the schedule will make the addicts (mostly asymptomatic) really vulnerable to withdrawal symptoms.

If you have started to feel an irresistible craving for something, however small or insignificant it may be, and are experiencing repining restlessness, then you are actually experiencing withdrawal symptoms. You are an addict! And an addict is a slave of his own habit!

Even an addiction of a silly sounding thing like poori-bhaji in Kishore Da's case, can be devastating, when he will be bereft of that thing for a continuous period of time.

A period of compulsory sabbatical, will give you the required will-power to overcome your addiction. You will be a rejuvenated individual when you would have learnt the ways of overcoming the pangs of the withdrawal symptoms of not doing something that was your everyday routine.

Just check whether that one irresistible impulse to eat something or do something is making you feel miserable.

That's the addiction virus. Sooner you get rid of it, the better it is for your mental health!

The Urge for Corruption

Yesterday evening, discussing some issues related to corruption. My friend in a WhatsApp group posted - I have seen corruption at grassroots level... In all small businesses and services. We can't blame only the Govt. or the top officials for corruption. The change has to start from us. But how??

I replied....

Absolutely right....

Change in collective mentality or collective behaviour is a very very slow process...

It is easier said than done.

To treat any malaise, we need to understand its causes.

I am reminded of a joke...

A school teacher scolded a small child and told him to call his father to meet her the next day.

Father in a very disturbed mood goes to meet the teacher. He asks - what happened? Please punish my son if he misbehaves or doesn't study. Don't spare him. Teacher said - nothing like that, I just called you to tell that he has been robbing things each day. Pencils, erasers, sharpeners etc. Students and parents are complaining. You tell me how to deal with him.

Father became furious, he couldn't ever imagine his son turning a robber....

He caught hold of his son's collar and yelled -

Why you need to rob such things, when I bring them from my office!

Many a times, we don't even realise what we are doing is **corruption**. Then where is the question of getting rid of it?

Simply saying we have to get rid of this corrupt mentality is not enough.

We have to deeply analyze what makes a person to commit corruption, only then we can do something in the direction of solving it.

The causes are lot many....

- Family reasons,
- Social reasons,
- Peer pressure,
- Office set up,
- Quick name and fame,
- Earning jobs,
- Undeserving promotion,
- Greed,
- Anger,
- Vendetta,
- Sadistic pleasure,
- Adventure feel,
- Desiring quick deity darshan,

- Addiction for bribery,
- Irresistible impulse for easy money,
- Natural wickedness,
- Weakness to possess material things,
- Medical or other emergencies,
- Simply fun etc.

First of all, we need to define corruption and only then we can do something to overcome it. It is normal to have a holier than thou attitude in such cases.

Gandhiji in his autobiography says - I used to attend high court to observe case proceedings and I used to sit on the last bench and invariably fall asleep every day. I felt very ashamed of sleeping in the court but my shame and guilt was lessened when I saw some more people sleeping in the last benches, giving me company.

That's what happens with corruption or bribery or malpractices, people feel less guilty as there are many to give them company. The remorse vanishes!

We need to bring too many changes in the upbringing of a child, altering education pattern, altering work culture especially in Govt. offices and so many other things and it is a damn slow process!

It is now so deeply rooted in our lives, culture and work ethics that it is difficult to have a single and quick solution to end corruption.

Nevertheless, somewhere a start has to be made!

Whom to Change And Why?

One of my friends recently suggested to watch a video of author Robin Sharma where he talks about change.

I saw the video and told my friend; I didn't find him telling anything new. He says people who are successful wake up early in the morning and use time fruitfully to build up their lives. I said this idea is as old as our Indian civilization. Almost 99% people in my villages in TN wake up at around 5 a.m. What's the big deal? The video hypes Robin's words, as if he has discovered some Theory of Relativity.

He tells bring change and be a change.

But from years that I have read about him. He has been doing the same thing; keep saying you can be the change or you can bring change.

Most people talk about how to be successful in business and end up selling books rather than doing some successful business themselves.

I have read another best-selling author who wrote how to make marriages work and lead a successful life. Later I came to know he himself has had 2 divorces.

Human beings have already changed the world so much. It has gone to dogs now!

I don't want to change it anymore. In fact, I want to leave it as it is.

Changing ourselves, changing the world etc. are all vague terms. Many so-called motivational speakers say things simply to please one section of corporate world people, who are simply making money sitting in cozy boardrooms, flying business class and attending useless seminars.

The Earth doesn't require we people to change it. It's powerful enough to change by itself. We occupy only a thin skin of crust and are actually powerless to change the composition of the earth; its mantle, core etc.

I would like people like Robin to give such flamboyant pep talks to hardcore terrorists and let's see whether they change.

Americans are different. Europeans are different. Africans are different. Japanese are different. And Indians are very different from all of them.

We find successful people in all the cities and all the countries with such diametrically opposite cultures and civilizations and economic development.

Change means who needs to change and like whom? And why?

Difficult to understand whom these motivational speakers want to change and why?

The Innocent Indian Wives!

Indian Wives know how much money is in their husband's pocket. They know which phone he uses. They want to know and control all that he does. They want him to go and do what she wants. But the moment he is arrested, they become innocent lambs!

They say they didn't know how he earned money, what he does outside the house. The conscience of Indian Wives seems to be pledged!

They enjoy the earnings out of the misdeeds of her husband's shady businesses but when he is arrested, he alone suffers imprisonment.

Why don't the wives file a FIR against their husbands and get them arrested in the first place?

Have you ever heard, a corrupt minister's wife or a mafia's wife or any wife of corrupt businessmen openly reveal anything?

No... Never!

Like some Bollywood actresses whose husbands were arrested for illegal businesses but they pleaded that they are innocent and never knew what their husbands did and how they earned so much money.

And above all they want us to believe that

The consolation that- Not all the people in the industry are such, is not applicable to Bollywood.

The fact that prominent Bollywood people are silent on the issue is a proof that -many are in the same Hamam!

It is just that the hypocrisy and sleaze of certain Bollywood people get exposed and others manage to escape the Sleuth's eyes!

Whatever be the outcome in any cases involving criminal husbands, corrupt husbands, mafia husbands, anti-national husbands etc. Indian wives will always wash off their hands saying - we are innocent and were not knowing anything about what our husbands did!

What a glorious life! As a wife you get to enjoy all the pleasures and luxuries out of the misdeeds of the husband but when the husband is caught, shamed and arrested, he suffers alone!

In spite of enjoying the fruits of unscrupulous deeds, wives are absolved and purged of all sins of her husbands!

You need, not just rational thinking to accept this but enormous gut in the spine!

Modern Housewives Salary Quotient!

When Geeta saw that her friend Reema always put up a happy smile, she asked-

Geeta: In spite of so much household chores how you remain so calm and cheerful?

Reema: That's because I like doing these jobs as I am paid for it.

Geeta: What do you mean?

Reema: Actually, you know my husband is a banker and a very reasonable man. So, one day, I said - I left my counselor's job to take care of children and also do lot of household work, my income became zero. I want to be paid for the jobs that I do for the family, after all the family is ours not just mine. It will give me financial independence and also give motivation to work at home.

My husband thought for a moment and said fair enough, we give 3000/- to our maid for the few work that she does. You do a lot more, so I think you should be paid 15000/- at least.

So, for the last few months I get a salary of 15K p.m. for being a home maker. I am very happy.

Geeta decided to take this idea to her husband who is an economic analyst at the CISR. She was beaming with joy on the prospect of earning at least 15K a month.

Geeta: Suniye, I left the job of a legal assistant and became full time homemaker to take care of our home and children.

Husband: Hmmm really, I respect your sacrifice and hard work.

Geeta: Respect and all is OK....But I think I have forgone my income for the sake of the family. The family is ours not just mine... Right?

Husband: yeah... What are you up-to?

Geeta: I want you to compensate my household work in the form of some salary.

Husband: (patient as ever) Hmmm makes sense. I am for it.

Geeta felt relieved and very happy.

Husband: But the point is how I will be able to decide what is the right amount of remuneration to compensate your work?

Let us sit down and work out a figure so that I can pay you every month.

Geeta: yes, yes sure

Husband: please get a paper and pen so that we can decide the monetary value of your contribution to the family.

Geeta brought the things with a calculator in a jiffy.

Husband (in analysis mode) Geeta you make a list of things that you do every day and also some work that you do once or twice a month... Accordingly we will put charges for that...

Please say...

Geeta starts...

Our Maid does clean utensils, sweeping, mopping and dusting etc... those we will leave out.

I do…

- Washing clothes in machine...Rs.1000

- Cooking food (2 times) ...Rs.3000
- Going to shops etc... Rs.3000
- Being at home to attend couriers, maid, receiving and sending children etc... Rs.6000
- Taking studies, orals, their HW etc. of two children...Rs.2000

Total comes to 15,000.

Husband: Very good. I too feel you should be paid 15K for being a homemaker and doing so many jobs.

Geeta: Grinning.

Husband: Geeta, do you know if I eat from office canteen...use office services...They deduct from my salary...

Geeta: yes.

Husband: We will make a list of the services or benefits or perquisites that you enjoy being a housewife and put a monetary value to that so that we will have a gross and net analysis of your work. And mind you it will be you alone who will decide the monetary value of the services not me... Ok

Geeta: Ok

Husband: I will go on telling the things, you write on this paper and you put a monetary value to that; finally, we will deduct that from your salary so that I will be able to pay the net amount.

Please also deduct the monetary value of the household work or services that I do for you that you could have easily done yourself.

Write down:

As you stay at home for most part of the day,

• Your share in maintenance...Rs.500

• Share in taxes....Rs.500

• Share in electric bill... Rs.1000

• Share in Dish TV bill as you watch for most part... Rs.300

• On Saturdays and Sundays, I do the vegetable shopping on your behalf...Rs.500

• My salary as your driver as on all sat and sun you make me drive to shops, temples, in-laws house, theatres etc... Rs.2000

• My salary for maintaining your two-wheeler...getting serviced, repaired etc. on Saturdays and Sundays....Rs.500

• Paying for your vehicle's petrol...Rs.1000

• At least on 2 or 3 Saturdays or Sundays we eat outside, remaining Saturdays and Sundays, I cook, so that should be deducted from your salary...Rs.1000

• Getting work done from plumber, electrician, getting ironed clothes from laundry (occasionally though) Rs.300

• Household cleaning on some Saturdays or Sundays...Rs.1000

• Picking up your relatives from station or airport (occasionally though) ...Rs.500

• Dropping and picking up of children from various Classes on Saturdays and Sundays....Rs.500

• Visiting vegetable markets and stores like D mart / Reliance Fresh and carrying heavy loads, once in a week…Rs.500

• Getting TV, fridge, AC, washing machine etc serviced periodically...Rs.500

• Supervising home colour work, gas repairs, furniture work etc. (occasionally though) Rs.500

• Your mobile bill, internet recharge etc... Rs.500

• On Saturdays and Sundays, I make online payments to electric bills, credit cards and do other online shopping for you...Rs.500

Still, we have not included -

• Your medical expenses...

• Your proportionate contribution to our family trip/ tour costs...

• Your personal shopping expenses...

• Your daily proportionate coffee, breakfast, lunch and dinner expenses....

• Value of various birthdays and anniversary gifts / celebrations etc....

Once we talk of paying salary to housewives, then we should talk of the value of the perquisites also that they enjoy being a housewife.

That may be correct in accounting and economics parlance but in family life it doesn't sound ethical.

Geeta (stunned and sad): You are right, I don't want any salary just give me some pocket money.

(Murmuring...never marry an economist...Baal ki khaal nikaalte hain)

I am reminded of one conversation that I had with a bhattji (priest) sometime back...he said this temple doesn't Pay me any salary. I am doing all the pujas for free.

I said: OMG! How do you manage your needs?

He said 'I am given free accommodation... Free food...free clothing and even they pay for my medicines...all the collection from devotees also they give me...but no salary.

I said these nothing but salary in kind. Please take a monetary value of these perquisites, you will know how much your salary is.

When people talk of housewives' role...They only talk emotionally.

They never take into account the explicit and implicit costs of being a housewife.

Although when we put a price for the work that are our moral duties, we actually belittle its sanctity!

Enlightening Insight from a Wife!

Vrinda worked as a marketing manager for the last five years. She always handled issues of men and matters with finesse. Very rarely one comes across any woman with so much patience and wisdom. Needless to say, she was the favourite employee in the office -rather a role model for other women in Multi-tasking.

She said she wished to throw a small party for her anniversary one Saturday after office hours. Seema casually asked - ma'am how many years it is that you are married?

She said -20 years.

Eyebrows raised in surprise. No one ever thought that she was married for two decades. Her personality was such - sealed at 30.

Again, Seema casually asked, now that you are living with your husband for twenty years, who do you think is important at this stage in life - Parents, Children or Your husband?

She didn't even think half a second - the answer was spontaneous, obviously my husband!

The expression in her juniors' faces suggested that they wanted her to justify or talk more about that.

What she said lingered in everyone's mind much after the day got over.

Sheer wisdom!

She said - I was married when I was 24.

It was an arranged marriage and I didn't know anything about my husband except that he was an Electrical engineer working in Tata Power. I didn't know his habits, mannerisms, his hobbies, his friends etc. At that point of time, it was a blind decision for me or rather for my parents. But such were the times in early nineties.

I joined this job and few months later I got married. At 24, I was a post graduate in commerce with a diploma in marketing. I knew nothing about life.

I was an average cook and didn't have any other talent to speak about.

My husband had immense patience about everything. He didn't mind any amount of mistakes I did. The very next year after marriage we bought a flat in Dombivli in 'Joint Name'. Later he bought me a two-wheeler in 'my name'.

He bought few ornaments as and when he would have sufficient savings or got any bonus. I was earning but he never used my salary to run the house. I had the freedom to spend my earnings as I pleased, to buy things for my parents and for my siblings too. He never cribbed!

We then bought our second home in Pune 'in joint name'. In fact, all my husband's bank account are in 'joint names'.

When I look back - It is amazing that he made me a joint owner to all the property and assets that he owns...all this I got from a man who knew nothing about me at the time of marriage.

My parents took care of me till I was 24, which was their responsibility anyway. After marriage, there was nothing from their side.... nothing even after their death. My brothers always argued - Vrinda is married now, no need of giving her anything.

At 24, I was still a naive girl. Just being in the company of my husband was a learning experience all the time. He gave me the exposure and freedom to tackle situations.... that I didn't get from my parents.

Unknowingly, we learn many things from the people with whom we live or spend time.... but because we would have spent first two decades in parent's house, we always tend to feel.... all that we do today has come from parents.

That's so belittling or trivializing the contribution of my husband in building up my life, personality and career.

It is not just unfair but cruel to credit everything to our parents - to say what I am today is only because of my parents - is an emotional cliché. That is unfair to a man who has given me so much time, energy, spent ten times more than what my parents did, took me on so many trips where my parents or brothers never took.

It is unfair to the man.... who has given me a status in the society, been there in all the activities of kids' upbringing. It is unfair to the man with whom I am going to spend my old age.

That's why I said my husband is the most influential person in my life!

What is true in my case actually may be true with many middle-class wives also, isn't it?

The female employees agree their respect for Vrinda madam increased many notches. And for their husbands too!

Issue of Food Wastage

Outwardly my heart agrees that we should not waste food while eating when so many in the world are starving.

But my mind says this is OUTRIGHT RUBBISH. Think over -

a. There is nothing as wastage...everything gets recycled....to mother earth it doesn't matter if we waste food...or anything...

b. By that logic...rich people have no right to earn so much money in business...stock market...investments and not to use them...when crores are living below poverty line... Mukesh Ambani lives in a 27-storey mansion with literally 23 floors vacant and wasted.

c. When resources belong to the nation how come we are allowed to waste 500000 billion liters of fresh water every day when potable river water goes down the seas.... when people are not getting pure water to drink?

d. In a country like India with over 10 crore unemployed youths languishing.... aren't the labour resources getting wasted?

e. Crores of rupees are wasted in making useless films which could be utilized for providing social security measures.

f. Every year India dumps nearly 30 million tonnes of foodgrains in the Bay of Bengal and we are talking of wasting a handful of food on our plate. How I not wasting food can provide food to the starving poor? They are starving not because of lack of food, its lack of education, job or money.

g. We have wasted the future of the whole country by electing hardcore scamsters and here we are talking about feeling guilty about wasting few food grains.

h. Look at how electricity is wasted in hoardings etc. when thousands of villages are still without electricity.

My grandmother once told me, 'when you finish eating leave some grains on the banana leaf' I asked her why? She said, 'when we clean up our leaf and throw it out at the roadside, the insects and organisms don't get anything to eat. So, leave something for them.' From then on, when I happen to waste some food unwillingly, I comfort myself by saying, I have left something for the other organisms. Even if we eat on steel plates today our wet leftovers somehow reach the organisms or mother earth.

Every day I see one gentleman buying biscuits for the street dogs and also putting grains for the pigeons near my society. I can say he wastes food because he doesn't eat what he buys but has he really wasted?

Next time if you inadvertently waste something, don't feel guilty. Think you have paid for and that has set the economy rolling. There is no wastage.

All that we waste when we waste some food, is our money. If we would have bought less, we could have utilized that money to buy some food for the next time. That's it!

Democrazy

A monkey laid its hands on a beautiful diamond necklace, by quirk of fate. Within no time the necklace was broken and scattered to pieces. The story is an apt peroration to what has happened to the freedom that fell upon India, some fifty years ago. Many intellectuals and rationalists are still in a state of shock as to how Indians dared to accept the administration of the country without any kind of prior experience. The worst thing to have happened in the annals of mankind is the timing of our independence. The country's population was around 40 crores (by no means accurate) and nearly 95% were illiterate as far as political science and democratic administration were concerned. Yet, our so-called messiah's of the freedom struggle had the guts to accept independence. They probably thought that the population our country will remain bolted and may not have dreamt of the extra 100 crore people in the next 75 years. Among others, Gandhiji thought Indians, especially the rural poor were very simple, straightforward, law abiding, selfless and very tolerant; so, it would not be a very difficult proposition to govern them. But sadly, what he didn't foresee is that such people are absolutely useless in a democracy; here people have to be exceptionally well informed and competent to make administrative decisions. Democracy is the most refined of all political order, so it can never be successful among asinine people.

Detached Or Insensitive?

I have heard and read about hermits, ascetics and seers spending years of deliberate meditation to achieve the 'Detachment Status'.

But the corona period has helped people achieve this in few months' time.

Many of our near and dear ones have died unceremoniously - without a proper funeral or cremation.

Since April 2020, invariably every morning a message arrives that so and so is no more. And that is just another number now!

In fact, people have been writing 'Please don't come for the funeral'.

News of someone's death is no more a 'mind rattling' or 'heart wrenching' one, it simply passes off without a whimper.

Suddenly we have been elevated to a higher plane of 'detachment' and that has come so fast without much effort.

Guests have dried up during festivals or birthdays or anniversaries. Students and businessmen are in a condition of stupor, not knowing how the turn of events will be in the next 6 months. Everyone's self-confidence is at stake!

People don't even have any time margin to mourn or feel depressed about someone passing away...the next news follows in quick succession.

Many great actors, cricketers, literature laureates and even some prominent politicians have gone in the last 15 months and people just brushed it like some other news from Somalia or Rwanda.

With the impending third wave or the fourth or the fifth, most citizens are going to experience the divine level of detachment from the worldly pleasures and relations.

Some may unknowingly label it as 'becoming insensitive' to tragedy.' But, treating bygones as bygones and moving on is a sign of 'detachment'.

During one such funeral recently, I struck a conversation with Mr. Yogesh, the person conducting the cremation. I saw him doing his job of piling up the dry logs and twigs so casually, that I felt he is nothing short of a 'Karmayogi' - not bothered about who has died or some people crying around him. It is just a job for him to consign many bodies to flames each day. If this pandemic continues for few more months taking many more lives, we all will achieve the saintly psychological status of 'absolute detachment.'

Adding Insult to Injury!

Ramakant was sitting on the floor in his 1RK and watching TV.

His wife as usual was lamenting and grumbling on the worst financial condition of their family in the last 18 months of corona lockdown.

Ramakant is a contract tailor and is now out of job. His eldest son is a chef in a small restaurant and now at home. His youngest son is a driver of a company bus, now at home as the company is shut down for good.

Needless to say, the little savings that they might have had got dried up. The mood in the house is charged with tension.

I have seen street urchins watching affluent kids eating pizzas, ice-cream and cakes outside posh eateries and there used to be so much pain and helplessness in their eyes.

The inequality in the standard of living in India is criminally alarming.

Ramakant looks at the TV ads of electric cars, luxury flats, study abroad, ornaments, Domino's etc. with a blank expressionless face, wondering for whom these ads are relayed in India.

Millions of families in India are already battered and bruised by the corona catastrophe, the TV ads catering to luxury desires of rich class, are absolutely undesirable at this point of time.

It is seriously adding Insult to Injury!

Next time when you see an advertisement of any luxury or expensive item on TV, just imaging what must be the feeling of viewers like Ramakant who are struggling for mere survival!

Poverty of Integrity!

For far too long... PSUs are operating as sick units... Sucking India's finance... In 1991 Manmohan Singh introduced disinvestment which was part of privatization.

It was he who wanted to privatize public sector enterprises. Of the seventeen industries, nearly 13 were privatized during his time, during UPA regime.

What Modi Govt. inherited was mostly loss making, grossly over employed companies.... How long those can be sustained??

It is like saying....

Mr. A was suffering from brain tumor.... local family physician first detected it... Gave some local medicines... Painkillers.... Referred him to a specialist.... The specialist kept him for few days, did various tests and sent him to a hospital with neuro-surgeon. He too made many tests. Meanwhile the condition of the patient deteriorated. The neurosurgeon referred to another super specialty neuro hospital where the tumor could be removed... The patient now reached the final fourth stage.

The surgeon said the chances of success are very slim... May be only 10%.... he went ahead with the surgery...The patient unfortunately died.

The patient was a local goonda politician...His mindless supporters came and ransacked the hospital saying the surgeon messed up with the operation and the patient should not have died.

The doctor was blamed and beaten up. Was he the one who killed him???

Many of our PSUs are like that tumor patient and Modi and co. are the surgeons treating the fourth stage patient.

And we are the mindless haters.

Change of Govt. is not change of system.... The corrupt system within every PSU and its nexus with the Govt. departments is an old malaise... Seasoned and hardened!!!

Top officials both in PSUs and Govt. machinery have brought this systematic rot in connivance which the erstwhile congress regime never made an attempt to plug. When select breed of individuals who don't have the slightest guilt or remorse of looting hard earned public deposits, are part of the banking sector, the country is morally bankrupt!

All the while we are saying education can only take the country forward. Mind you, all the scamsters too are so called educated white collar criminals. If our education only creates bankers who embezzle, doctors who run patient looting rackets. Professors who trade internal marks for money so on and so forth. We actually don't want people to get educated. They are far more dangerous to our country than rural simpletons.

While we bash a roadside pickpocket black and blue, we treat these star criminals with respect. That is the sorry state of affairs.

Education has failed us...

Banks have failed us....

Govt companies have failed us....

Courts have failed us....

Above all politicians have failed us!!!

I am reminded of a Kishore Kumar classic song from the Amar Prem movie...Lyricist Anand Bakshi says - Majhdhaar mei naiyya dole toh maajhi Paar lagaye, majhi Jo naav duboye Usse kon bachaye!!!

Fixing Answerability!

It is a common Indian trait to make someone in the post or power to make answerable or responsible for everything.

It is seen at all levels.

Take the case of our small co-operative housing society, all the members of the society feel for all the things happening in the society, the managing committee is solely responsible -for all the problems it is only the managing committee that is answerable. Now what is the harm if other members participate in finding solutions? But no-no-no... non-committee members will act as if they are in opposition and the managing committee are the ruling party.

This is seen also at state level and national level.

Is it a rule of nature that only the ruling party should solve all the problems due to natural calamities in the state?

What's the harm if the opposition BJP helps in taking some steps???

But it is the mentality of the masses that we will only hold the people in power responsible for everything.

This is also reflected in people's habit of blaming PM Modi for everything.

I think this is a sign of an immature society; we still have to go a long way to rationally understand that running a country is not just the ruling party's job but also of all the people and political parties.

And every problem that we face is not just the responsibility of the party in power to solve but also of all the parties that claim to serve the people.

Simply criticizing, is the opium of the people not in power, it can make you feel vindicated when the Govt. doesn't perform or fails in solving an issue but it can never provide solutions.

At times of crisis, the opposition should score brownie points by helping people and helping the Govt. find solutions, it will surely give 'vote-dividends' during elections.

Government's Public Spending

It may have happened with us all.

We all have some tea cups at home---may be 5/6 or 7 cups.

Suppose someday some 10-12 friends happen to come to our house, we have only 6 cups, we use some tumblers or glass or even bowls.

One of the friends' remarks - लाखों का घर लेते हैं पर दस- बारह कप नही लेके रख सकते? फालतू में टीवी , कार पे खर्च किया पर कप नही खरीद सकते ???

Things in anyone's house will always be in proportion to the usual number of members at home or may be few extra.

Just because there are 30 guests for marriage in our family in a particular year, we cannot have 30 beds in spare always.

When we have money do we buy a car or we buy an ambulance???

Please think.

The problem is similar.

People say why so much was spent on Sardar's statue or stadium? Why not any hospitals?

Just imagine we constructed 100 more hospitals in a town. Six months down the line, the pandemic gets over.

The hospitals will then go vacant or underutilized. What will you do then with those structures?

Emergency situation is a special situation. Everything else would seem a waste during such times.

No doubt infrastructure has to be developed but that doesn't mean everything else is useless.

In India any amount of infrastructural development will soon reach its saturation if people continue to have children in wholesale numbers.

State Control of Hindu Temples - Fundamental Rights violation?

Before we discuss the case in point-a quick reference is needed to some relevant articles so that the premise becomes clear.

Article 14:

Guarantees to all, equality before law and equal protection of laws. The President and the Government are an exception to the equality mandate.

Article 15:

Prohibits discrimination against any citizen on ground of religion, race, caste, sex or place of birth of any of them. This article was amended by 93rd Amendment, 2005 for providing reservations to SCs, STs and Backward Classes in private unaided educational institutions.

Article 25:

Prohibits freedom of conscience and free profession, practice and propagation of religion, subject to public order, morality and health.

Article 26:

Provides freedom to manage religious affairs.

Thousands of temples having assets worth thousands of crores in many states especially South Indian States had been taken over by the government.

Supreme Court in 1954 struck down the "illegal" provisions of the Madras Hindu Religious and Charitable Endowment Act 1951 related to the appointment of executive officers in temples, but the same provisions were brought back by legislating the Tamil Nadu Hindu Religious and Charitable Endowment Act in 1959.

When we correlate and extrapolate the essence of the 1959 Act with the said Articles 14,15,25 and 26, the Act itself seems to be in violation of Fundamental Rights of Hindus.

Now the appeal is not to the Hindu community. The other religious community if they claim to respect and obey the constitution, then they should prove that in spirit, by fighting for the rights of Hindus to free the temples from the clutches of the Govt.

There is no reason whatsoever to fear that the Hindu temples assets will be squandered or misappropriated once it goes out of Government's hand, if that was the case why the Ram Temple at Ayodhya was handed over to The Trust?

The Clarion call is not for the Hindus to rise against this 62-year-old Act but for the people of other religions to stand up to the cause of equal treatment to be meted out to the religion of the Majority.

If they really mean and care to uphold the Fundamental Rights then they should join hands with Hindus in 'Decentralizing and Disinvesting' the Hindu temples!

Much Ado about Nothing!

Tamil Nadu has a culture of its own - a civilization much older than even Roman or Egyptian. The glorious part is that it is still perpetual and the worst part is that the 'racism' element is also still evident - both the people and the Govt. have not grown up!

DMK was built on Atheistic views - that's fine.... but since the current Govt. came to power, the hatred for Brahmins at all places and all levels is visible. It is slowly building up into ostracization status and then it may putrefy and become something like 'Hatred for Jews' during Nazi times in the late thirties. Before the situation explodes into ugly proportions, the civil society, the intelligentsia and the central government should take serious cognizance of this 'Reverse Apartheid' towards brahmins in TN.

One case in point -

Suresh Raina (celebrated CSK player) was commentating in one T20 match and while saying that he loves TN culture and has some close friends in TN, he said he too is a brahmin. In the context of the conversation, by saying he is a brahmin, he actually meant he also feels he is a part of TN.

Now the social media (instigated by Brahmin haters) goes berserk and cries foul against Suresh Raina.

In a land where every caste people beat their chest to claim reservation from the Govt., it is the Brahmins who have never asked for any reservation in spite of actually being in minority.

Forget about any favors from the Govt. can they not even say they are Brahmins???

Why should the Brahmins be forbidden from saying they are Brahmins??

Are they asking for any reservation??

TN is setting a bad precedent. The hatred for Brahmins that is slowly brewing since the time Stalin became CM has to be nipped at this stage.

The Brahmin haters are finding more opportunities to vent their hatred more than ever before.

The feeling of vendetta was always simmering, as the DMK kept it fanning from the times of E. V. Ramaswamy, it props its ugly face from time to time!

I don't see anything objectionable; Brahmins too have a right to call themselves Brahmins and also feel proud about it. It is not a crime!

Role of the Almighty

Of the many things that keep rattling my mind is the role of God in the scheme of things.

Is he the creator of the grand design or a part of it?

Many questions that keep lurking in the recesses of the brain come to the fore especially at times of enormous calamity like the corona virus pandemic.

I must appreciate that corona virus is truly secular and genuinely apolitical.

It has made its presence in Muslim countries - UAE, Pakistan, Iran etc., Christian countries - Italy, Spain, USA, UK, Germany etc... And of course, Hindu dominated country - India.

The Gods of various religions have collectively failed to nip the problem at the bud stage. Lakhs of people are in its grip and still counting.

At times such as these, we cannot stop asking ourselves, what exactly is the role of God in this world?

Religious puritans who have donned the role of a lawyer to defend God's position might say it's is all God willing. It is an act of balancing; God is a great leveler! OMG....then why the hell we are taking measures to stop the Act of God... We are actually inviting and intimidating his wrath.

Then there will be so called astrologers who might say things like rahu is in Mithun Rashi so world is seeing disasters etc., if it is a part of a natural planetary course, simply leave it, why bother?

Some fatalists even go to the extent of saying some Chinese groups were doing the sin of eating all sorts of animals, from Wuhan wet markets so God chose to punish them.

But in that case why we are punished? Just because we buy Chinese products, have we become a part of their sin?

When thousands are reported killed by the virus onslaught, I feel it is nothing short of a war effect! All these years, countries were struggling for nuclear non-proliferation to save civilians life and here we have a silent war by the Chinese on the world killing thousands without being blamed by the world for have started a virus spread -nothing short of a biological war in disguise.

Over hundred countries are paying for the foolishness or lackadaisical attitude of the Chinese Govt. for not curbing the problem at the initial outbreak stage. It allowed the world to suffer.

After the First World War, Germany was made to pay through its nose through the treaty of Versailles. But today China is left Scott free!

Sooner or later this problem will subside but if wet markets continue to thrive in China, we are sure to have many more new generations of viruses that will cause widespread economic losses and human sufferings.

I don't believe that human-created Gods have any clue about what's happening in the world now, let alone providing a solution!

The Delusional Claustrophobia

On April 14th 1912, when the Titanic was hit by a small upper part of an iceberg on the right bow of the ship, small blocks of ice flew up sprayed and fell on the upper deck.

At the first look, the passengers jumped in joy, some got their hockey sticks out and pushed around the ice pieces along the wooden floor...simply enjoying their unexpected joy that the sudden shower of ice presented. Their joy was only short-lived.

Never in their wildest dreams would they have imagined that the invincible Titanic will sink within the next few hours.

More than hundred years later, China, Italy, Spain, Germany and US did the same mistake of not heeding proper attention to the corona outbreak in the initial days and it swelled into catastrophic proportions as it progressed to the third stage.

But these countries barring China, still have a small size of population and will very well tide over the challenge in a couple of weeks' time but when I come to think of India. I get nightmares!

It is very difficult for any Govt. administration in India to convince people to be self-disciplined. People get a unique high to do things which are odd, queer and anti-establishment especially not following Govt. advisories for the betterment of public safety and security. Over the years, on many issues concerning our society or nation, not following the protocol is the strict protocol here. It is akin to Teenage syndrome where guys and gals would purposely do the things that are expressly told as forbidden. Our whole country has that behaviour!

People who otherwise languish like a couch potato lying in one corner of the sofa for most part of Sundays like a buffalo in a cool mosquito ridden puddle, suddenly start trembling with claustrophobia when our PM ask them to stay at home for a day.

A couple of days of self-quarantine or confinement or restraint is the least that we can do to help the cause of arresting the chain of corona spread.

If few days of forced rest at home gives us a feeling of imprisonment, just imagine how people like Swatantra Veer Savarkar would have felt in an 8 X 6 ft. dungeon in Kala pani for 10 long years.

I spitefully despise the arrogant and 'above the law' behaviour of some of our so-called Bollywood celebrities...who always want to tread on ways that are detrimental to the larger interests of the nation... Thereby they want to appear special.

Yes, special anti-social brats!

Let us condemn their hypocrisy and not emulate them in any way.

The corona virus iceberg has already hit our great Indian Titanic.

Let us not take this lightly and allow the ship to sink.

Let us douse the fire before it engulfs the whole nation and goes beyond state health machinery's control!

The Appeal in the Repeal!!!

It takes a different acumen to understand Indian politics. The more we delve into it, the more we get stuck up in its mire.

The repealing of the 'Three Farm Laws' will go down as a classic case for many things.

I am sure the year-long agitation will be remembered as a 'Sordid Saga' - if at all people have any memory beyond news headlines.

A 1996 Mumbai case I remember, a brother - sister duo fought a case for the property against their father and won the case. The court's order that the ancestral property belonged to the grandchildren, rendered the old father homeless. The children celebrated the legal victory; in other words, they celebrated their father's defeat. Father remained a destitute and died after few months.

The case remained in my memory - a case where I still cannot decide whether the children won or they actually lost. The case got reminded, when I saw yesterday the opposition was celebrating the 'Repealing of Farm Laws' as the victory of the farmers or agitators.

No doubt it is the victory of the agitators but in the process, too many bad precedents have been set as a fallout of this repeal-

1. The repeal has shown that even if laws are properly passed by following the parliamentary procedures, it can still by struck down by hostile agitations by a group - that's a dangerous precedent for the future. Then what use is following the parliamentary procedures when a group can get the laws repealed by arm-twisting tactics.

2. If the agitators are extremely happy with the repeal, which indirectly means that they are very happy with the existing laws....and they gave the impression that all the hell will break loose if the three laws are implemented. Therefore, there is no need for any reform for the next 100 years. Now definitely farmers cannot complain about their sufferings or getting exploited by the prevailing laws which they didn't want to change anyway.

3. The agitating farmers mainly from Punjab assumed they have been appointed to represent the entire farmers' community of India. While we saw there was actually no support from the majority of the farmers elsewhere in the country. There is a real danger that this formula is going to be repeated in near future.

4. The agitating farmers proved - that they can survive a year-long agitation....and that shows poor farmers of Punjab are actually not poor. They have the highest PCI among farmers in India.

5. The Govt. learnt a lesson, it need not bother about amending or introducing laws, people are happy with status quo.

6. Any layman can understand there have been some external 'invisible hands' which provided the support for various disruptive activities in the Farmers' agitation. This was precisely the thing that few days back NSA Ajit Doval said as the fourth-generation warfare - issues being raked up to create unrest in the civil society.

Democracy won at the cost of democratic process.

The analogy that comes to my mind is — a severely diabetic patient's leg was amputated to save his life.

Now he doesn't know whether to be happy being saved or miserable that he won't be able to walk again.

Whatever be the political compulsions of Modiji- Amitji in repealing the Farm Laws, it has at least shown that the Govt. is open for roll-backs and can buckle under public pressure.

The eyes of the anti-national elements both outside and inside will be lit up at the prospects of pulling down the Govt. The fact remains 'the repeal' has set too many bad precedents that will linger for years to come whether this decision has solved any security concerns or has exposed new security challenges only time will tell.

The Slow Death of Our Collective Conscience?

Our Indian society has a collective conscience or at least we believed it had.

But with 24 X 7 rampant social media at work, our conscience or the lack of it is thoroughly getting exposed.

Just few months back in Maharashtra, we had One Home Minister

One Police commissioner

One top level cop wielding their power swords as if they were the truthful custodian of our dignity and safety and today, they are in jail-their corruption, high-handedness and crimes thoroughly exposed.

What will be their fate in the next few months is anybody's guess.

We should not be bothered whether they will serve rigorous imprisonment or be hanged, more serious issue is how we general populace reacted to the arrests of these high-profile individuals.

We simply took it lightly, just brushed aside the news as if it was another daily weather report.

It had to be the gravest matter in any civilized society, the HM, police commissioner and top cop who are elected or appointed for safeguarding law, themselves are such hardcore corrupt people and indulge in such organized crimes. Even the word 'Shame on us' is mild. Did the HM work as an individual? Was he one man in his party? Why he is singled out?

While corruption in political parties in India is organized and collective, the moment a bigwig is caught in the law net, all others in the party distance themselves as if they are purged of all sins by some holy milk bath. We have seen it in umpteen cases in the past.

Same in the police department, the tainted commissioner didn't work as an isolated individual, so when he gets caught, shamed and jailed, all others simply remain aloof of the issue.

We as common people, the voters, have never felt ashamed of being ruled by such unscrupulous politicians. No morchas, no dharnas, no rasta-rail roko for such serious issues- it is just another story for us.

We are more bothered about what saree an actress worn for her son's birthday or whether a cricketer looks good on beard or which new bike he has bought. We even get enraged if some caste issue is mentioned in some Tamil film.

But we are absolutely not bothered about what kind of people we have as our HM or police commissioner; anyway we never expected any integrity from any politician. Even the ruling parties feel no remorse for what their minister or high-ranking officers did, let alone taking any action against them.

Such is the height of apathy of us Indians to serious political issues - the slow death of our collective conscience is clearly visible or is it already buried???

Using Democratic Right to Kill Itself.

Recently I came across a proverb in Hindi -Tezaab ussi bartan ko galata hai jisme usse rakha jaata hai. It translates as - acid dissolves the same vessel which contains it.

Interesting, isn't it?

This fits well for our Indian democracy too.

Indian democracy gives a right to protest and the methods adopted to exercise it, is killing the spirit of democracy.

I am not against any protest but the manner in which JNU students did it or rather do it time and again, is grossly despicable to say the least!

They don't even seem students forget about being educated.

Being an Educationist for over three decades, I have witnessed protests for fee hikes over the years from parents but it was all very decent and law abiding. Parents were taken into confidence and the management justified the fee hike.

There are rules and limits for fee hike for a single time, if JNU or any other educational institution for that matter takes to unreasonable and unjustifiable fee hike then there are legal recourse available. Vandalism and hooliganism and sloganeering have no place in an educational institution.

Modi Sarkar may be monstrous. It may have killed the spirit of free education. But still the students don't have the right to desecrate swami Vivekananda statue and writing anti saffron graffiti etc.... This is stretching too far and clearly underlines the role of non-university actors.

When JNU or any such institutions were giving facilities at peanuts cost all the past decades, never the students appreciated them.

And now they are creating a huge ruckus. There are over 1000 universities in India and it cannot be that none had ever hiked fees or service charges in the last few decades. But we have never come across any JNU type protests.

The fact that police has to be called every now and then in JNU campus indicates that there is a section of students who have agenda and ulterior motives and the administration has every right to wield an iron wand to thwart such disruptive activities.

I have personally seen quite a few Students Organizations' protests (backed and instigated by a political parties) at many places, over the years and I can tell you the students used to be brought in trucks and that lot never seemed to be students interested in studies. They were outright hired goons.

Many poster boys of protests whom we see on media, never seemed to me like students who have come there to study. They are over aged and simply want to have political mileage; they have nothing to do with students' welfare.

If we are to justify and stand by what the Students did in JNU...Then we should support rail roko...buses jalao...school ko aag lagao... whenever there is a fare /fee hike.

Whenever there is an increase in our society maintenance we should burn down our society office and beat up the secretary.

In the last thirty years, the price of Masala Dosa has gone up from Rs.12 to Rs.120 but, we want JNU to charge only 10 rupees for a room per day. As for the argument that 40% students in JNU are literally beggars and can't afford the fee hike, that is far from truth. If they are so poor then education is actually free for them or there are scholarships and NGOs to take care of them. That is no justification for the mindless methods adopted by them to protest.

I am not justifying the fee hike or the method adopted by the administration in implementing them, but I condemn the manner in which the students reacted; that is unworthy of students who have come there to study.

There are people who want everything free in our country - Free electricity, free train travel, free education, free housing, free medical, free this and free that. This is against the basic economic principle of circular flow of GDP.

While it is plain economics that if the Govt. suffers a loss by way of subsidy, it will have to be compensated elsewhere or the Govt. will be caught in a deep debt trap within no time!

In the words of noble laureate Mohammed Yunus (Champion of Grameen Bank and Inclusive growth) we should enable ways to strengthen the financial capabilities of the poor so that they can pay for what they get. Freebies are economic termites. But in India all Governments without exception have thrived on such unviable populist schemes and used it as a crutch to scamper through the five ruling years.

The poor should be alleviated and made to feel proud that they are capable of paying for food-clothing-shelter at least. To accept anything free or even at subsidized rates is a dent to the self-respect of any civilized individual.

We all want top class services without being ready to pay for it.

JNU is no different!

From Right to Pray to Fight to Pray

India is a funny country with funny controversies. For people with humorous eyes can see the fun everywhere even in theological controversies.

Recently, one of my Malayalee friends asked me whether I have ever visited 'Sabarimala Shrine' in Kerala. I said I never felt the urge or fascination to see Lord Ayyappa as yet. But still he wanted to extract my take on the age-old tradition of not allowing women in the age bracket 10 -50 to see Lord Ayyappa. I thought my friend's wish was weird for he knows very well that I am not quite a friendly commentator on issues involving religion.

The feeling to do something that is forbidden is an irresistible itch in humans. It is rather a teenage syndrome which we carry through our lives although its intensity decreases with age.

People will diligently go and touch the gate if there is a board 'wet paint, don't touch,' teenagers will try smoking and drinking if there is a strict 'Farmaan' at home against it. If a nondescript film is banned on some flimsy reason, then it surely runs to packed houses for a few weeks. There are so many commonplace examples to exhibit our compulsive behavior to do restricted things. That's what some women activists want to do - try to do something that is forbidden. It gives a sense of victory, an intoxicating high to go against the establishment and claim moral victory -read spiritual victory in this case.

Respecting certain religious practices and honoring Human Rights or providing for gender equality simultaneously is actually an impossible task. It is something like balancing atmospheric pressure, temperature and humidity at a given place - there will never be a time when all three would be equal.

What are now Hindu religious practices in India and elsewhere are nothing but rules made by people and definitely not by God. They are time specific that is to say - they were logically convincing at the time when they were conceived and implemented originally. If women perceived the restriction as a draconian condition, then it wouldn't have survived for centuries.

This is neither a problem nor a rule made to vilify women. That's actually the beauty of Hindu religious practices. Every famous temple has its own set of requirements and rituals different from others that adds an element of spice and excitement to the devotees.

Like black mund or waist cloth has to be worn at Sabarimala...men must enter Guruvayur Temple shirtless... you have to tie red chunari to invoke goddess Vaishnodevi...wear particular style attire during puja or worshipping sessions.... abstinence for 40 days to visit certain shrines...then there are special mantras to be chanted which are exclusive to deities...tonsuring of head in some temples, so on and so forth. So, restrictions are not restrictions they are actually peculiarities of that shrine. It is indeed fun obeying them and making it a human rights or gender inequality issue spoils the uniqueness or USP of that shrine. Almost all the temples have one or the other restrictions like opening and closing timings, type of special offerings for different temples, even dress codes for devotees etc. While in most temples, people in inebriated condition are not allowed, we have some temples where liquor is the main offering to the God or Goddess and even chickens are sacrificed at the altar. We have never objected to such diametrically opposite rituals in different temples and it has been followed without any complaint or revolt for millennia.

That is again the beauty of Hindu religion in general and temple rules in particular. This is where Hindu religion differs from other major religions of the world and hence what applies to other religions doesn't apply to Hindus. For instance - Most churches and mosques have structured and codified method of administration and worship and they also follow their superior authority for decisions on festival dates and other celebrations, while there are no such things in Hinduism. The anarchy in Hinduism is to such an extent that even a roadside beggar-turned baba gives discourses on Hinduism and there are scores of morons following him.

There are so many temples in India where women have exclusive domain and men are not allowed to enter either at all times or at selected times.

To name a few -

Kamrup Kamakhya Temple - Guwahati, Attukal Bhagwati Temple - Kerala, Chakkulathu Kavu Temple - Kerala, Bhagwati Maa Temple - Kerala, Jagatpita Brahma Temple -Rajasthan and other Santoshi Mata Temple where men are prohibited from entering the temple on Fridays.

Have men ever staged a protest raising a gender issue in the above temples? They have simply respected the rituals and are happy with other temples where they can worship.

In the case of Sabarimala Rule-

If all women felt offended or mortified with such restrictions then girls below 10 and women above 50 would have stood in support and boycotted the shrine. But that didn't happen all these centuries. Even mothers of girls below 10 years send their daughters with pride, fully knowing that they themselves can go only after reaching 50. By and large most young women are happy about not being allowed to enter Sabarimala because they have grown up knowing about it and don't actually see it as any human right violation or gender inequality.

Any attempt to rationalize these things through court intervention is preposterous because there is no single authority in Hinduism to say what is right and what is wrong and there is no proper code of conduct for neither the temple authorities nor for the devotees. On what basis will the court decide when rules and rituals for Ganesha temples, Vishnu temples, Shiva temples, Devi temples etc are so very different? Even makeshift temples during Kumb-Mela, Sarvajanik Ganeshotsav in Mumbai and Durga temples during Navratri in Kolkata have their own manner of conducting pujas and have some restrictions on devotees. The court cannot give any ruling based on any established Act or legal sections or provisions, neither it has any precedence of this kind to settle the Sabarimala issue.

I think the court should not entertain such cases where special conditions or restrictions of certain temples are involved.

On a lighter note - The Supreme Court should follow this Sabarimala Shrine practice and issue a Diktat - People coming to us to settle such issues are prohibited from entering Supreme Court premises!

Thick Skinned Conscience!

The recent brouhaha in many Indian states over usurping or grabbing power is nothing but a reflection of times that we are living. Degeneration of moral values is a very lighter term for the happenings that we witness in recent times.

Political scene is just a reference and small point in the whole picture.

Jewelers with brand identity are systematically running a racket and cheating people - selling adulterated gold and fake diamonds and bogus Ponzi schemes.

White collar crimes by bank management are tumbling out almost every week; people's trust is crushed and their providence in saving is decimated.

Not to talk of builders cheating home buyers.

While such cases of mass cheating and dishonesty and corruption are brought to light, I feel these are not one-off cases. When I seriously observe the dealings of servicemen like plumbers, carpenters, electricians, motor mechanics etc., I have found very few of them are actually honest and trustworthy.

For instance -The materials promised by them are not used, unnecessary replacement of parts, over billing and unreasonably high labour charges.

Even in other cases, we know of diagnostic centers and medical shops offering commissions or cuts to doctors making referrals. Then there are bribes for tenders in govt. contracts etc. You name a field and examples galore of cheating and malpractices.

Even in relationship today, trust is easily broken and people don't have the slightest remorse for having deceived or back-stabbed someone like their spouse, kin, friends etc.

We are not feeling shameless or guilty because there are so many to give us company in the shameless acts.

Two parties go into pre-poll alliance and later cheat people by splitting. The so-called leaders don't even have an iota of guilt that they have actually thwarted people's trust and mandate.

Right from a job of smaller position to any top job you may imagine, it is sad to see people getting used to this shamelessness for some quick material gains.

We are insulating our conscience with such thick skin so that our immoral and unethical deeds don't prick it!

The Language Politics

Many linguists in our country opine that 'Hindutva' feels Hindi is superior to other regional languages'.

Their observation and surmise is rather childish and their fear irrational.

What an irony that we are ready to accept a foreign language English in all the states but not ready to accept an Indian language Hindi.

Come year 2200, believe it or not all the languages which don't change with time will slowly perish.

English will by default become official language and Hindi, the colloquial language for conversation.

It takes centuries for languages to evolve or perish.

However, we may claim Sanskrit to be a Godly language; can it be a local language for communication or can it be official language for business?

Over a period of time, People automatically will adopt the language that is convenient for them, you cannot impose any language on anybody.

Why most Maharashtrian families prefer to put their children in English medium schools? Even the ministers who take vote citing Marathi Asmitha, put their children in English medium schools. Why?

Because that is with the times.

We may or may not accept it but it is a fact.

Did the Englishmen put a gun on parents' head to put their children in English medium schools? Or did they forcibly impose on us?

What is true to Maharashtra is also true to other states.

Hindi has nothing to do with Hindutva, if that was the case then tomorrow linguists will say all the Hindi songs composed, all the films made in Hindi were to promote Hindutva.

South Indian states simply hate Hindi for their vested political interests. Nothing else!

I would like to ask, what are the criteria to determine the superiority of a language? If anyone can state the conditions, it will be easier for us to rank the Indian languages accordingly and decide their superiority quotient.

Politics And Conscience

Recently one minister resigned stating that his conscience forced him to take high moral ground.

When allegations were levelled against him some 15 days back, he stubbornly refused to budge. When the courts hit the knuckles, he is taking high moral ground in his resignation.

People very well know that Indian politicians and conscience are totally aliens.

If people had any moral values why they would be politicians in the first place.

Fooling the people and taking them for a ride was very easy in 70s and 80s but Indians in 2025 are smartphone people and social media users.

It is better that the politicians understand that their Hypocrisy-game is over and out.

By the end of this decade no politicians would be able to hide his ill-doings and mafia practices, it seems only those politicians with clean track record will survive.

Amen!!!

The Failed Population Policy

During his first official visit to Allahabad in 1947, Jawaharlal Nehru spoke about his intense wish to implement a population policy. He was shocked to find instant criticism to his views. In a country where children are considered as gifts of God, any policy attempting to limit man's right to procreate would be condemned prima facie. Nehru quickly gauged the repercussions of his population policy and wisely in his political interests decided to divert his attention to agriculture and other fields. Thus, the seeds of indifference were sown immediately after gaining independence. Population policies since independence have been wayward, blunt, half-hearted and grossly unsuccessful. If our Family Planning Measures and other programmes had been successful, our population today would not have been 1.4 billion. The irony of the situation would yoke anyone; the implementation of the family planning measures restricted the families of the educated class while the families of the illiterate and poor families swelled unprecedented. This has led to a situation where families, which can afford to bring up many children, are with one or two children while poverty-stricken families have children by dozens. This has defeated the purpose of all our Family Programmes and has left our country in a lurch.

What our country needs is a red-hot iron wand to whip up those who come in the wake of 'compulsory' family planning measures. The governments in every state should have the spine to persecute the couples who violate the policy and arraign them. For that to happen we need a communist mentality in us; some sort of a wolf in sheep's clothing. When so many political parties, so many ethnic groups, so many classes and so many conflicting ideologies have to thrive, it is very difficult to formulate any Population policy with some mettle. Thus, any population policy announced hereinafter is eyewash and only another economic proposition that will result in wastage of money, materials and manpower.

Divide And Rule

Before the advent of foreigners, India was a land of more than 600 kingdoms. It is very difficult to digest that the kingdoms were in friendly terms and it was only after the coming of the British that the unity was broken with their infamous doctrine of 'divide and rule'. What is truth will be very difficult to digest, especially for a prejudiced patriot. The truth is that all the kingdoms existing in India always waged war with one another to expand their kingdom. Their cultures and ethnic background were so very different that there was no question of unity. It is a well-documented fact that a foreign country coined the word 'India' to the land on the other side of the 'Indus River'. History suggests that all the racial groups prevalent in India have migrated from other continents, hence, it is a ridiculous idea trying to establish the identity of the original Indian race. Therefore, a question of dividing the country does not arise when there never was a single country as such. More so, those were the times when subjugating other kingdoms, provinces or regions was the order of the day. People who came later in chronology to this country have been branded as foreigners while those who have come few decades earlier have become our countrymen (notwithstanding their plundering and vandalism). This is absolutely preposterous.

A random appraisal of the administration of the Indian Government since 1947 will bring to light so many instances when our government has resorted to divisions. Starting from dividing our country into linguistic provinces, our politicians have divided the country on the basis of religion, caste, class, etc. Each mother political parties have got divided into several sub-parties. The difference between the haves and have-nots has become unscalable. All and sundry divisions that have taken place since independence was for the sake of administrative convenience and to establish a socialistic pattern of society, that is what is the justification of the Government. But the same, when done by the British is claimed to have been done to divide the people and sow the seeds of hatred among them. This double standard defies logic. The fact is 'divide and rule' was not a policy of the British but is the tenet of good administration. It is decades that the Britishers have left our country but we still keep harping on the same string. People harp because their knowledge and interpretation of our history is poignant and wretched. The politicians harp because they can't survive without 'divide and fool'.

www.ingramcontent.com/pod-product-compliance
Lightning Source LLC
Chambersburg PA
CBHW022158160726
48282CB00024B/240
9788198221544